W9-APG-544

HIDDEN HISTORY
SPIES

Harriet Tubman

UNION SPY

by Jeri Cipriano
illustrated by Scott R. Brooks

RED CHAIR ·PRESS·

Hidden History: Spies is produced and published by Red Chair Press:
Red Chair Press LLC   PO Box 333   South Egremont, MA 01258-0333
www.redchairpress.com

Publisher's Cataloging-In-Publication Data
Names: Cipriano, Jeri S. | Brooks, Scott R., 1963- illustrator.
Title: Harriet Tubman : Union spy / by Jeri Cipriano ; illustrated by Scott R. Brooks.

Description: [South Egremont, Massachusetts] : Red Chair Press, [2018] | Series: Hidden
   history: spies | Interest age level: 008-012. | Includes sidebars of interest, a glossary, and
   resources to learn more. | Includes bibliographical references and index. | Summary:
   "The story of Harriet Tubman and her role in leading slaves to freedom along the
   Underground Railroad is well-known. But did you know that during the Civil War
   Harriet would often dress in disguise to gain important information to share with the
   Union Army?"--Provided by publisher.

Identifiers: LCCN 2017933812 | ISBN 978-1-63440-284-2 (library hardcover) | ISBN 978-1-
   63440-290-3 (ebook)

Subjects: LCSH: Tubman, Harriet, 1820?-1913--Juvenile literature. | Spies--United States-
   -History--19th century--Juvenile literature. | United States--History--Civil War,
   1861-1865--Secret service--Juvenile literature. | CYAC: Tubman, Harriet, 1820?-1913.
   | Spies--United States--History--19th century. | United States--History--Civil War,
   1861-1865--Secret service.

Classification: LCC E444.T82 C56 2018 (print) | LCC E444.T82 (ebook) | DDC
   973.7/115/092--dc23

Photo credits: p. 7, 8, 28: Library of Congress; p. 29: Lvklock; p. 32: Courtesy of the author,
Jeri Cipriano; p. 32: Courtesy of the illustrator, Scott R. Brooks

Map illustration by Joe LeMonnier

Printed in the United States of America

1117 1P CGBS18

Table of Contents

Chapter 1 A Dangerous Mission

hree war boats sailed down the river. The boats carried 150 black soldiers who once had been slaves. They were making a sneak attack on the enemy in South Carolina.

It was a dangerous job. The enemy had put underwater bombs in the river. At any moment, a gunboat could blow up!

The soldiers had to surprise the enemy. They had to destroy bridges and supplies before enemy soldiers could fight back.

The boats moved quietly in the fog. Slaves saw the gunboats and became scared. They started moving away from the river.

Then one boat moved closer to shore. A tiny person stood on deck and started singing. The slaves stopped moving away. They knew that song. They recognized the voice as a "call to freedom."

Suddenly, hundreds of slaves turned and ran for the river. Women ran with babies in their arms. Children hung onto their skirts. Hundreds of slaves, young and old, splashed into the water. They couldn't swim. But they would make a break for freedom, or die trying.

Soldiers worked quickly. They kept pulling slaves up into the boats. They had to make a quick getaway—and they did.

The mission was a success! The gunboats carried more than 700 slaves north. In the North, they would no longer be slaves. They would live as free people.

Harriet, the Conductor

Who was the "brain" behind this bold mission? Who planned the attack? Who chose the troops and trained them? The leader was a top war spy for the United States government. Her name was Harriet Tubman.

Harriet had a lot of "spy" experience. She had led slaves to freedom long before the **Civil War** broke out. Harriet was a *conductor* of the **Underground Railroad**.

Spy Moves

Sometimes Harriet wore disguises for trips. She might dress as a man or an old woman. Tubman always met the slaves on Saturday nights. This would give them a head start. Newspapers did not print lists of runaway slaves until Monday morning.

Secret Codes

People of the Underground Railroad used everyday words to speak in a secret code. Many words used were railroad terms.

Agent The person who planned the escape route and made contacts

Baggage or Cargo The runaway slaves

Conductor The person who led slaves to freedom

Heaven Freedom

Station A safe house

Stockholders People who donated money, food, and clothing

Moses The name people called Harriet Tubman. Like Moses in the Bible, Tubman led her people out of slavery.

The Underground Railroad was the code name for people who helped slaves travel secretly to the North to become free. The work was top secret. Conductors sent secret messages to slaves in different ways. One way was through songs.

$200 Reward.

RANAWAY from the subscriber, on the night of Thursday, the 30th of Sepember.

FIVE NEGRO SLAVES,

To-wit: one Negro man, his wife, and three children.

The man is a black negro, full height, very erect, his face a little thin. He is about forty years of age, and calls himself *Washington Reed*, and is known by the name of Washington. He is probably well dressed, possibly takes with him an ivory headed cane, and is of good address. Several of his teeth are gone.

Mary, his wife, is about thirty years of age, a bright mulatto woman, and quite stout and strong.

The oldest of the children is a boy, of the name of FIELDING, twelve years of age, a dark mulatto, with heavy eyelids. He probably wore a new cloth cap.

MATILDA, the second child, is a girl, six years of age, rather a dark mulatto, but a bright and smart looking child.

MALCOLM, the youngest, is a boy, four years old, a lighter mulatto than the last, and about equally as bright. He probably also wore a cloth cap.   If examined, he will be found to have a swelling at the navel.

Washington and Mary have lived at or near St. Louis, with the subscriber, for about 15 years.

It is supposed that they are making their way to Chicago, and that a white man accompanies them, that they will travel chiefly at night, and most probably in a covered wagon.

A reward of $150 will be paid for their apprehension, so that I can get them, if taken within one hundred miles of St. Louis, and $200 if taken beyond that, and secured so that I can get them, and other reasonable additional charges, if delivered to the subscriber, or to THOMAS ALLEN, Esq., at St. Louis, Mo. The above negroes, for the last few years, have been in possession of Thomas Allen, Esq., of St. Louis.

WM. RUSSELL.

ST. LOUIS, Oct. 1, 1847.

Posters like this one were put up all around an area when slaves ran away. Many offered a reward for their capture.

Harriet made 19 trips back to her home state of Maryland. On each trip, she protected her "baggage." *Baggage* was the secret code name for slaves who were escaping to freedom. Harriet reached these slaves through song. Her call to meet her was the song "Go Down Moses." If she sang slowly, the coast was clear. It was safe for the slaves to run to her in the deep woods. But if she sang loudly and quickly, she was giving a warning: "Go back. Go back. You are being followed. It's not safe yet."

The journeys were very dangerous. Sometimes slave catchers with dogs would follow the runaways. Harriet knew safe stops along the route. A *safe house* was where people fed the slaves and let them rest. Sometimes they hid the slaves if slave catchers were too close. Harriet's first trip was in 1850. She worked as a conductor for ten years. She led 70 slaves to freedom. And no one was ever captured!

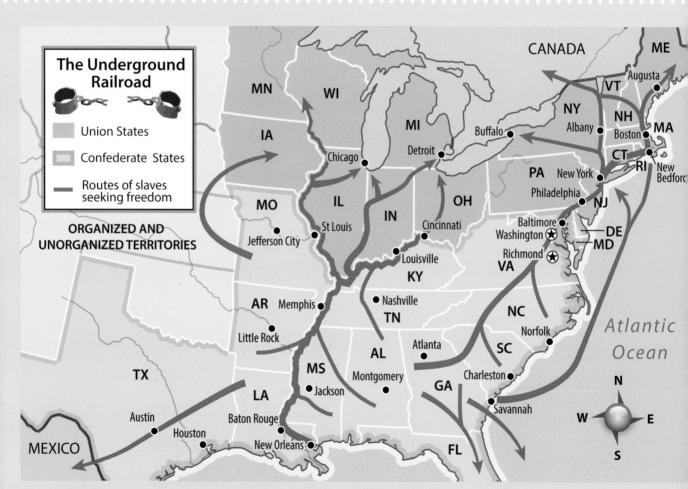

The Underground Railroad passed through 14 states and into Canada.

Harriet Tubman, Dead or Alive

In the late 1850s, slave owners offered a $40,000 reward for catching Harriet Tubman. Back then, $40,000 dollars was equal to a million dollars today! One day, she overheard some men reading her wanted poster, which stated that she was illiterate, or unable to read. So Harriet picked up a book and pretended to read it. The trick was enough to fool the men.

The Underground Railroad was active for ten years. It stopped when the Civil War broke out in 1861. More than 1,000 slaves escaped to freedom through the Underground Railroad.

War Breaks Out

The United States went to war in 1861. It was a war like no other. This war was called the Civil War because U.S. citizens fought each other. What caused neighbors to fight? The main reason was slavery.

Southern states had slaves working on large farms called **plantations**. They wanted to keep slaves as slaves. Northern states had just voted with President Lincoln to end slavery.

Harriet Goes to War

When the Civil War broke out, Harriet joined the **Union Army**. She wanted to help free *all* slaves, in the North and the South.

In 1862, Harriet went to Beaufort (*BO-fort*), South Carolina, to be a nurse. That is where Harriet met Colonel (*KER-nel*) James Montgomery.

Union Army soldier

Confederate Army soldier

The uniform a soldier wore showed which side he was fighting for.

Montgomery saw that Harriet made a good spy. He trusted her to plan and lead the attack on the Combahee (*KUM-bee*) River in 1863. He also counted on her to find, train, and work with other spies.

Harriet knew that slave women would make great spies. Owners did not think slave women mattered. They did not pay attention to them. Owners did not think slave women knew anything. Most slave women could not read or write. So owners talked freely in front of slave women. They told each other secrets in front of the women.

But slave women heard everything. They saw everything. They remembered everything. The slave women told Harriet what they heard and saw. They told her where soldiers hid along the Combahee River. They told her where to find the underwater bombs.

Harriet, The Spy

Harriet became the first woman in American history to lead troops into combat. She used many tricks she had learned on the Underground Railroad.

Harriet often wore disguises. She also learned to be in the right place at the right time.

Once she dressed as an old woman and went to a police building. The police were holding a runaway slave. They would be sending that slave back south to his or her owner.

A large crowd of black people gathered outside the police building. From a window, the old black woman gave a hand signal. The crowd ran into the building. They fought with the police and freed the runaway slave.

People say Harriet Tubman was the "old woman." She was really a very young woman at the time.

Some Lady!

How did Harriet Tubman support herself all the years she worked in the army? She made and sold pies!

Later during the war, the Union Army asked Harriet to find and train black men as spies. She became head of the whole information-getting business. She also led raids into slave territories. She persuaded slaves to leave their masters. Then Harriet helped them join troops of black soldiers as fighters and nurses.

Women: Secret Warriors

In the mid-1800s, American women were "second-class" citizens. They had no legal rights. They couldn't vote. They couldn't work at the same jobs as men.

Some women found ways to be treated equally. They disguised themselves as men. They would do men's jobs and earn men's pay, too.

Spy With Healing Powers

Harriet also worked as a nurse during the war. Soldiers got wounded in battle. They also got sick. Harriet knew how to cure many illnesses. She used secrets her mother taught her. She knew how to find plants that had healing powers. She used these to nurse soldiers back to health.

During the Civil War, close to 1,000 women disguised themselves as men and joined the armies. Soldiers who joined the Union Army got $152 just for joining. That was half the yearly salary of most workers. Soldiers got regular pay, too.

Not all women joined armies to better themselves. Many joined to fight side by side with their husbands.

Chapter 2 Harriet Tubman, The Early Years

Nurse... Cook... Spy... Fearless Leader... How did Harriet Tubman come to be all these things? What was her life like as a young child growing up?

Harriet Tubman was born into slavery around 1822 on a plantation near Bucktown, Maryland. She was named Araminta, or "Minty," for short. She was the fifth of nine children of Harriet "Rit" Green and Benjamin Ross, both slaves.

"There was one of two things I
had a right to: liberty or death.
If I could not have one,
I would have the other."

Harriet was whipped daily as a little girl. She had to work in icy cold waters setting muskrat traps. Life was hard. One day, the master sold three of her sisters. Harriet never saw them again.

Harriet was hired out to different masters. Some were very cruel. When she was about 12 years old, Harriet was hit in the head with an iron weight. The blow broke her skull. The injury caused her problems the rest of her life. She would fall asleep at any time and in any place.

When she was older, Harriet was hired out to a shipbuilder. She showed great strength and energy, working like a man.

The owner agreed to let Tubman hire herself out. She paid him a yearly fee of sixty dollars to work for herself. Soon, she had earned enough money to buy a pair of oxen. The oxen helped Harriet earn more money. Why did she work so hard? Perhaps she was dreaming of buying her freedom one day. Harriet hated slavery.

Like Mother, Like Daughter

Harriet "Rit" Ross was a strong woman. That's why Minty took the name *Harriet* as an adult. It was a way to honor her mother.

Harriet's mother showed Harriet how to be brave. She taught her to stand strong for what she believed in. "Rit" Ross had lost three daughters when they were sold away. She wasn't going to let that happen again.

Then her master had a plan to sell her baby boy. Rit hid the boy in the woods for a month.

One day, the master came to her cabin. He looked very angry. Rit faced him boldly. *"You are after my son; but the first man who comes into my house, I will split his head open,"* she said.

It was a standoff. Neither the master nor Rit backed down. Finally, the master left. He gave up plans of ever selling another of Rit's children.

Marriage

Around 1844, Harriet married John Tubman, a free man. Because Harriet was still a slave, any children she might have would be owned by her master. The children could be sold or given away.

When the master died in March 1849, Harriet knew she would be sold and could end up further from the North. Harriet decided to make a break for freedom before it was too late. Then she learned that John was not planning to join her in the North. He had met and married a "free" woman and was staying in Maryland.

As Harriet made her way through forests and fields all alone, she was met by kind men and women who helped her move from one safe place to another until she was in Pennsylvania—and freedom! In Philadelphia she got a job as a dishwasher and met **abolitionists**, people who wanted to end slavery. The abolitionists told her how the Underground Railroad worked to help slaves escape to freedom.

She put her mind to freeing family and friends.
From 1850 to 1860, Tubman returned to Maryland
many times to rescue slaves and lead them along
the *railroad*.

Chapter 4

Harriet Tubman: The Later Years

In 1859, Harriet bought a small home in Auburn, New York. She moved her parents and other family members there.

Harriet was always worried about money. She decided to earn money by giving speeches. She spoke at Women's Rights meetings and at anti-slavery meetings. She called herself "Harriet Garrison" to avoid the slave catchers.

A Difficult Trip

In 1857 Harriet made one more journey, her most difficult. She returned to Buckstown to get her elderly parents. They were too old to walk far, so she hid them in a wagon and drove all the way from Maryland to freedom in Canada.

After the War

After the war, Harriet retired to Auburn, New York. In 1869, she married Nelson Davis, a war veteran.

Although Harriet was well-known and respected for her work, she was very poor and close to penniless.

Harriet never got back pay for all her spying during the Civil War. But she got a widow's pension as the wife of Nelson Davis. Then, in the late 1890s, she got a Civil War nurse's pension.

Harriet continued to do good works. She donated a piece of her land to build a Home for the Aged near her house. In her last years, she moved in there herself. She worked for women's rights until her death at age 90.

Honoring Harriet Tubman

In 1944, during World War II, a Liberty ship was named for Tubman. It was the S.S. *Harriet Tubman*, the first ship named for a black woman.

The U.S. Postal Service made a Harriet Tubman stamp in 1978. In the 1990s, Harriet's brick home in Auburn became a **historic landmark** and has a visitor's center on the land. In 2013, the Harriet Tubman Underground Railroad Byway in Eastern Maryland opened. Visitors travel the route to see important places from Harriet's life.

Harriet Tubman was a tiny woman who grew to be a mighty warrior. Her story of courage continues to inspire people in the United States and around the world.

Got Change?

A new $20 bill is being prepared to honor Harriet Tubman. It will show her face on the front. Harriet will be the first woman and the first African-American to be on U.S. paper money. The change is even more important because she replaces President Andrew Jackson, a slave owner!

After a fire in 1886, Harriet's house in Auburn, NY was rebuilt in brick. It still stands today.

Glossary

abolitionist a person who wants to get rid of slavery

Civil War a war between different groups of people within the same country (The United States Civil War lasted from 1861–1865.)

Confederate Army the army of the Southern Confederacy, the South, during the Civil War

historic landmark a building or monument that has national importance and is a national symbol.

plantation a large farm where crops such as cotton and tobacco are grown.

underground railroad a network of people who secretly helped slaves from the South to free states in the North or Canada before the Civil War.

Union the states that remained loyal to the federal government during the Civil War; the North.

Union Army the Army of the North that fought to keep the United States together.

For More Information

Books About Harriet Tubman

Bauer, Marion Dane and Tammie Lyon. *My First Biography: Harriet Tubman*. Scholastic, 2010.

McDonough, Yona Zeldis and Nancy Harrison. *Who Was Harriet Tubman?* Penguin Books, 2002.

Weatherford, Carole Boston and Kadir Nelson. *Moses: When Harriet Tubman Led Her People to Freedom* (Caldecott Honor Book). Hyperion, 2006.

Books About the Underground Railroad

Coleman, Wim and Pat Perrin. *Follow the Drinking Gourd: Come Along the Underground Railroad*. Red Chair Press, 2015.

Lassieur, Allison. *The Underground Railroad: An Interactive History Adventure*. Capstone, 2007.

Places

The Harriet Tubman **Home**, Auburn, New York

The Harriet Tubman **Birthplace** and **Museum**, Cambridge, Maryland

The National Underground Railroad **Freedom Center**, Cincinnati, Ohio

Index

About the Author and Illustrator

Jeri Cipriano has been a children's writer and editor for many years. She is the author of more than 100 books and served as an editorial director of classroom magazines at Scholastic. When Jeri is not writing, she enjoys taking photographs of people and places.

Scott R. Brooks started a career in full-time illustration several years ago. Scott shares his Atlanta, GA studio with his illustrator wife, Karen. They share their home with their 2 clever children, and their somewhat less clever dog and cat.